THE
HALL OF FAITH
SERIES

Courage
That Changed
The World

THE EXTRAORDINARY HISTORY
OF THE KNIGHTS OF ST. JOHN

D0639674

BY RICK JOYNER

MorningStar Publications
Division of MorningStar Fellowship Church
P.O. Box 440, Wilkesboro, NC 28697

For a free catalog of MorningStar Resources,
please call 1-800-542-0278.

Courage
That Changed
The World

Part 1
Fearless Warriors

The exploits of the Knights of St. John during the Middle Ages are some of the greatest stories of courage, endurance, and steadfast devotion to a vision since biblical times. Three times, a small band of a few hundred knights took their stand against the most powerful armies of Islam. Outnumbered by as many as a hundred to one, they vowed not to retreat before the enemies of the cross, and they held their ground. Although they endured some of the most terrible sieges and human wave assaults in the history of warfare, when the smoke cleared, their flag was still flying. They simply could not be dislodged from the ground they had claimed.

To the world's astonishment, the little band of the Knights of St. John stopped the unstoppable hordes of Islam, and Europe was saved. To this day, the "Knights of Malta," as they came to be known after one of their most famous battles, are still celebrated in many nations for their great courage that changed the world.

Before they fought these epic battles, the nations of Europe scorned those in the Order of St. John as "archaic relics from the past." Christian rulers denied them supplies and reinforcements. No one gave them a chance against the huge, modern armies of Islam, and none of the rulers of Europe were willing to waste forces or supplies trying to help them. Still, to become a Knight of the Order of St. John, one had to vow never to retreat before the enemies of the cross. They determined to die rather than yield a single acre of Christian land to "the infidels." Most would die, and every single knight would be wounded, but they never retreated. The great nations of Europe that scorned them soon stood in awe of their courage and their victories. Monarchs publicly acknowledged that these brave souls had saved them from the conquest of Islam.

Though the weapons of our warfare are not carnal, but spiritual, there are great and timely lessons to learn from the amazing history of the Order of St. John. Epic battles such as they fought must be waged today in the spiritual realm. Great knights of the Spirit are gathering again, vowing to never retreat before the enemies of the cross. They are taking their stand against the greatest powers of darkness now covering the earth. Although these powers seemingly are succeeding at building their strongholds of deception and corruption in every nation and culture, once again brave knights of the Spirit are gathering to take their stand against these hordes from hell. They are building their own strongholds on truth, honor, and true spiritual chivalry. If we are to prevail, our fight will require the same courage, endurance, and focused vision as that of the Knights of St. John.

THE CLASH OF EMPIRES

Islam was founded on the theology of jihad, which is a Holy War to conquer the world by force for Allah. War is glorified in Islam. Since death in jihad guarantees Muslims a place in heaven, regardless of their previous sins, the most esteemed men of this religion are those who prevail in battle. Muslims believe that when the religious leaders proclaim a conflict to be a jihad, the doors of heaven open to admit those who give their lives for the cause. Multitudes have seen jihad as their opportunity to gain heaven in spite of their debauchery, and so they actually hope to die in battle. This makes the warriors of Islam some of the most deadly and fierce soldiers that the world has ever seen.

Initially, Christendom in the Middle Ages had quite a different perspective on war and warriors than did the Muslims. Peace was seen as holy, while wars and warriors were both considered necessary evils. This viewpoint put the Christian West at a distinct disadvantage when confronted by Islam. Eventually, popes changed the church's policy toward war and chose instead to sponsor the Crusades. They began to foster the belief that religious adventurers could gain eternal glories for their participation in such conflicts against "infidels." For almost two centuries, from 1096 to 1291, wave after wave of Christians swept across the Middle East in crusades to recapture the Holy Land from Islam. This conflict did not end with the Crusades, but the Crusades actually laid the foundation for the strife that continues in the region to the present time.

Although Muslims are fearless warriors, prior to the Crusades, they generally treated Christians with honor and were sometimes even generous with their defeated enemies. They showed a considerable degree of religious tolerance in the lands under their control and permitted followers of the Lord to visit the Christian shrines. The Eastern European Christians were also tolerant of Muslims, even allowing a Muslim quarter and Mosque in Constantinople, one of the greatest cities of Christendom at that time. Of course, both sides committed numerous atrocities, which always occur when men take the battlefield. Even so, an unwritten code of chivalry and mutual respect generally prevailed in the conflict between Islam and Christendom until the 12th century.

As the Crusaders laid siege to Jerusalem in 1099, the Muslim governor showed remarkable consideration to his Christian subjects, even allowing them to leave the city to join the Crusaders. However, when the Christians finally breached the walls and conquered the city on July 15, the bloodlust and cruelty of the Crusaders was so great that even the most battlehardened soldiers who heard of it were appalled. Muslim men, women, and children were promised clemency if they would stand under the Christian banner set on a hill after the walls were breeched. Instead of clemency, they were surrounded by the Crusaders and slaughtered by the thousands. Seeing this, the entire Jewish community fled into the synagogue. The Crusaders sealed the doors and then torched it. Not a single Jew survived. Then the Crusaders, covered in the blood of their victims, came weeping to the tomb of Christ thanking God for their "victory." But it was surely hell rejoicing that day, not heaven.

The mosques, including the Dome of the Rock, were plundered. Forever destroying the unwritten code of chivalry that existed in the conflicts before that time. For centuries to come, the Christian "victory" in the conquest of Jerusalem would be one of the darkest clouds hanging over the church. On that day, any trust the world had in the church was shattered, and it has not yet been recovered.

A NEW ORDER OF WARRIOR HEALERS

Nearly twenty years before the conquest of Jerusalem in 1088, a Catholic monk named Brother Gerard founded two hospices for pilgrims in Jerusalem—one for men and one for women. These became the world's first hospitals and he dedicated them to St. John the Baptist. Godfrey of Bouillon, the first Christian governor after the conquest of Jerusalem, made a gift of land to the hospices. As the conflict with Islam continued, later rulers of the city made it a custom to give these hospitals a tenth of their spoil.

In 1113, the pope recognized the servants of these hospitals as an independent Order, dubbing them the Order of St. John. As the conflict between Islam and Christendom escalated, the Order was soon forced to establish a new branch of service to the pilgrims—a military arm devoted to their protection from bands of outlaws that roamed the land. Although they were to become forever famous for their military exploits, the Order of St. John never forgot that their first mission was to serve the sick and wounded. Thus, warfare and healing were combined in one of the most unique spiritual Orders ever created.

After every battle, when many of the combatants would be fainting from exhaustion, the Knights of St. John would remove their armor and serve all of the wounded on both sides before resting. In order to maintain humility and focus on their original commission to serve the sick and oppressed, every member, including the Grand Master himself, spent time regularly serving as an orderly in one of their hospitals. To this day, members of the Order are referred to as "Hospitallers," and are esteemed internationally for their charity and service to the sick and oppressed.

Throughout history there has been an ongoing debate concerning whether times make the men or men make the times. While there can be a good case for both sides of this argument, in regard to the Order of St. John, it was clearly the times that made the men. The Order was thrust into a vacuum created by the situations and events which surrounded them. Even though their primary calling was to serve the sick and oppressed, they took their stand as warriors because the times required it. They fought simply because they believed it was the right thing to do.

Since the knights did everything they set their hands to with all of their hearts, they accomplished far more than they had ever envisioned or planned. Although there was not a single great military genius in their ranks, they won seemingly supernatural victories by simply keeping their word. Just as they refused to retreat from the ground they had taken, they also refused to retreat from honor and chivalry. Thus their hearts were united with their deeds, and these truly noble men defeated the most powerful armies on earth.

THE CONFLICT SPREADS

Until the 13th century, most of the conflict between Islam and Christendom had taken place in the Middle East. The Byzantine Empire headquartered in Constantinople provided a formidable shield to any Islamic ventures into Christian Europe. However, to the consternation of the pope and the Christian kings throughout Europe, the fourth

Crusade to leave Western Europe marched into Constantinople, sacking and destroying it in 1204.

Pope Innocent III condemned the Crusaders outright. The attack on Constantinople by these Crusaders proved to be not only one of the most despicable acts in history, but also one of the most foolish. The Eastern and Western churches would forever be divided, profoundly weakening the Christian West, and the shield that Constantinople had provided against Islam was destroyed.

The Crusades continued to fall into such debauchery that even their victories horrified Christendom and led to further disintegration and disunity. Of course, this opened the door even wider for Islam. The Crusaders' cruelty during their victories eventually led to devastating defeats as the fortunes of Christendom universally reversed on the battlefields with Islam.

When the Crusades finally ended in almost total disgrace, the Turkish Ottoman Empire became the most powerful and cultured empire in the world. After conquering the Middle East, much of Africa, and Eastern Europe, the Turks stood poised to sweep over the rest of Europe. The remaining

Christian nations of Europe were consumed in political and religious wars with each other and they could not raise a common army to stand against the Turks. It appeared that nothing could stop this tidal wave of Islam from completing its subjugation of the world for Allah.

A NEW HOME

Almost the entire garrison of the Knights of St. John in Jerusalem had died as the last Christian defenders of Palestine. The only survivors were a few of the wounded who were carried to ships in the harbor. The stories of the valor with which their brothers fought and kept their vows to never retreat, galvanized the resolve of the remaining knights of the Order which was still based in Europe. Together, they found a home on the small island of Rhodes, where Rhodian sailors, famous throughout the centuries for their seamanship, instructed the knights in their nautical skills. The knights learned quickly and soon became known as the most capable mariners in the world.

As the Eastern and Western churches divided and fell into constant quarrels within their own camps, Islam was unifying under brilliant and able leaders. Meanwhile, the Order of St. John prospered during these times, becoming wealthy from the booty of the Crusades and from what they captured through their constant raiding of Muslim ships and caravans. Although they were not by any means totally exempt from the corruption and politics of the day, as Christendom was increasingly distracted by conflicts within, the Knights of St. John remained unified and remarkably focused on the enemy without— the Turks and the increasing threat of Islam.

Rhodes was situated precariously in the middle of Muslim shipping lanes throughout the Aegean Sea. However, the knights considered this to be a convenience rather than a problem. They quickly made themselves odious to the Ottomans with the boldness of their raids. For 150 years, the Knights of St. John were so effective in their sea battles that the Turks were prevented from developing their own naval power. This was the only thing that prevented the Ottomans from pursuing their conquest of the rest of Europe, since their supply lines were continuously broken by the seafaring knights.

The knights also worked continually to improve the fortifications at Rhodes. As divisions and internal conflicts eroded Europe's power, the pope's repeated call to arms against Islam fell on deaf ears. At the same time, one of the most distinguished leaders in history, Mehmet, was unifying Islam. He was a brilliant man, fluent in a half dozen languages, who possessed extensive knowledge in literature and science. He quickly raised the cultural, economic, and military excellence of his people to a level which surpassed the nations of Europe.

Meanwhile, the little Order of the Knights of St. John was scarcely more than an annoyance to the Ottomans. Although the Order was considered to have no real military power except for their naval skills, they were able to slow the advance of the mighty armies of Islam, which had no equal on earth.

Mehmet was a conqueror who fashioned himself after Alexander the Great. He marched on Constantinople and subdued the great city. Europe then stood before his army like an open treasure chest. Even so, he realized that he could go no further until he did something about the knights on Rhodes who continued to plunder his shipping and supply lines. In 1480, Mehmet sent his most able generals and an army of 70,000 men to subdue the 600 knights at Rhodes. The knights assembled another 1,500 to 2,000 local militia to stand against the coming onslaught. Christian Europe, seeing no hope for the Order against such odds, refused to send them reinforcements or supplies. No one expected the siege of Rhodes to be more than a very brief event.

THE FIRST BATTLE OF RHODES

After landing his great army with little resistance, Mehmet's siege cannons began to batter the walls which the knights had spent over a century building. Numerous other cannons hurled projectiles over the walls into the city. The Grand Master of the Order was a Frenchman named d'Aubusson. He was a remarkable leader with great foresight who had prepared his knights for the siege he knew would one day come. He had even built shelters for the townspeople so they could escape the bombardment. Knowing they could expect little or no help from Europe, d'Aubusson nevertheless determined that they would not abandon a single acre to Islam as long as they could draw a bow or wield a sword. He was true to his word.

After days of bombardment, in early June the first wave of assault troops attacked the Tower of St. Nicholas, an outlying fortification of the city. The Muslims were shocked by the stiff resistance they met, and were driven back, suffering many casualties. As their anger rose, they followed this attack with another general bombardment, hurling more than a thousand cannon balls a day at the city for several weeks.

Gradually the walls of the city began to collapse. The Turks snaked closer and closer with their trenches. So many fires burned throughout the city that the knights who fought on the walls by day had to fight the fires at night. Those who were present at Rhodes declared that a scene out of hell itself could be no worse. But still the knights refused to surrender or retreat.

On June 18, the Turks launched a second major assault led by the fearsome Janissaries, renowned as the greatest fighters in the world. Each Janissary was chosen at the age of seven because of his physical potential and trained his entire life for combat. They were forbidden to marry or engage in any kind of family affections in order to focus all of their emotions and energy on battle. They had never retreated or been defeated in battle, and the whole world expected their assault to be the final end to the little Order of St. John.

The Janissaries came under the cover of darkness, expecting to find the knights sleeping. To their surprise, the knights were at their posts waiting for them. The sound of gunfire and clanging swords filled the night until dawn. When the sun arose, an amazing scene was revealed. Multitudes of Janissary bodies were floating in the moats around the tower of St. Nicholas. The Turks looked up in stunned amazement to see the knights still standing defiantly on the battered walls.

The Turkish generals had never experienced such a military setback. Resorting to subterfuge to pry the knights from their fortress, they planted agents in the city who pretended to be defectors to the Christians (many of the Sultan's troops were captives from Christian nations). These spies were soon able to do great damage and created serious tactical problems for the Order.

The weary knights were pressed from within and without. Each day seemed to present a new crisis that threatened to be their doom. The fortifications were crumbling everywhere, and the worst breeches were at the most strategic points. Still the knights refused to yield. When the Turks began massing for a final great assault, both sides fully expected it to be the end.

A FIGHT TO THE DEATH

Many weeks of constant bombardment had nearly reduced the entire city and its defenses to rubble. The few remaining defenders had very little protection from this great rain of death. Still, they held on. Finally, to the relief of both sides, on July 27 the last great assault began. The knights and the remaining militia took their positions. The Sultan sent his bashi-bazouk troops first. These were mercenaries who were considered expendable and indeed they were expended, as countless waves of troops were cut down by the defenders.

The bodies of the bashi-bazouk troops soon filled the ditches and streams, making human bridges that lead up to the walls. This had, in fact, been the strategy of the Turkish generals all along. The tired and wounded defenders watched as great waves of the fearsome Janissaries arose and began their advance. They were now more determined than ever to destroy the remaining defenders because of their previous humiliation.

The Turks quickly overwhelmed the strategic Tower of St. Nicholas, which had taken the brunt of the main assault for nearly two months. The knights contested every acre of ground, for which the Turks paid dearly as the ground was covered with their dead. D'Abusson, with an arrow in his thigh, led a dozen knights and three standardbearers up a ladder and onto the wall where the Grand Master received four more wounds.

Then a Janissary "of gigantic structure" hurled a spear right through d'Abusson's breastplate, puncturing his lung. He was dragged back out of the fray just as the enemy made a breach in the defenses and began to pour into the city by the thousands. It appeared that the end had finally come for the Order of St. John.

In possibly the worst hell that men could create on earth, the Turks continued to throw themselves against the remaining knights with wave after wave of fresh troops. In hand-to-hand combat over burning rubble, the tenacity of the knights and their ability to inflict casualties astonished the Turks, and started to dismay even the angry Janissaries.

As the battle reached its most critical point with the final breakthrough seeming but seconds away for the Janissaries, suddenly above the smoke and turmoil of this terrible inferno, d'Abusson's standards appeared on the last remaining parapet. He was held up by three bearers in shining armor who appeared almost as gods from the hell below. The effect on the Muslims was electrifying. A wave of fear swept through the assault troops and then spread throughout the entire army. The remaining bashi-bazouk troops fled in terror that overcame even the Janissaries. The entire Turkish army began to melt away in confusion, retreating at the very moment when total victory was easily within its grasp.

As the Turks fled, Rhodian sharpshooters climbed the walls and poured a deadly rain of arrows into the retreating army. Amazingly, the remaining knights found enough strength to counterattack, chasing the pride of the Sultan's troops all the way to their base camp. Within ten days, the shattered army that had been the prize of the Ottomans fled the island. The whole world was stunned by the outcome. The Order of St. John had not only survived—they had prevailed.

AVOIDING A DANGEROUS VICTORY

Both Scripture and history verify that the most devastating defeats often follow a great victory. Two well-known examples of this are the biblical battle of Jericho and the first American Civil War battle at Manassas. After destroying the seemingly impregnable fortress of Jericho, Israel was humbled by the little village of Ai. Likewise, military historians believe that the Confederate army could have easily captured Washington, D.C. after their first victory at Manassas. However, they became so disorganized because of their celebrations that they could not follow up the victory, thereby losing their best chance to win the war.

After the Knights of St. John's imminent doom was miraculously turned into a great victory at Rhodes, their relief and rejoicing must have been very hard to contain. Yet they immediately went to work preparing for the next great assault which they knew would certainly come. This was characteristic of the Order's brilliant leadership during the most critical one hundred years of its history. They kept their focus on the bigger picture of winning the war rather than on just winning a single battle, regardless of how spectacular the victory had been.

The decimation of the seemingly invincible Turkish army by such a small force was viewed as a military miracle of biblical proportions. The Order that had been viewed by Europe as "an archaic relic of the past" was elevated to a new prominence. Some even called them "the saviors of the continent." Even so, the surviving knights did not attribute much importance to their new renown. Somehow they already sensed that it would not result in any substantial help from Europe for whom they were so desperately fighting. Even so, they were not laboring for renown or reward, but because they considered it their sacred duty to stand against the enemies of Christendom. As soon as their wounds healed, they began with renewed resolve to rebuild their fortifications, restore their weapons, and rigorously train for battle. It was that kind of will that caused them to become some of the world's greatest warriors.

By their defeat at Rhodes, Islam was held in check. They could not advance into Europe while the knights held the little island and continued to attack their supply lines. While all of Europe celebrated, the knights knew that their victory had made them even more odious to the Sultan. They knew that Europe was by no means secure after just one battle, and they were bracing for Mehmet to send an even greater force, which is exactly what the angry Sultan planned to do. The knights knew it would be many years before they could be ready for his retaliation.

The Lord must have heard their prayers, for on the Sultan's way south through Asia Minor, he became sick and died, causing the expedition against Rhodes to be canceled. Because of Mehmet's death, the knights had more time to repair the walls and recruit reinforcements before the next onslaught. With this reprieve, they began to feel they might have a chance to successfully stand against the next onslaught. Fittingly, even d'Abusson survived his wounds.

As soon as he recovered enough to resume command, d'Abusson began preparations for the next battle with characteristic devotion. It was as if he knew that the whole world's destiny had been cast upon his shoulders. The money received from Europe was devoted to the reconstruction of the walls and towers, as well as the purchase of munitions to be stored for the next siege. As it turned out, the Ottoman Army of the Crescent would not return to Rhodes for forty years. It would take every bit of that time for the knights to prepare for what was coming, and they used it wisely.

D'Abusson died in 1503, but his vision and leadership insured that the fortress at Rhodes would grow even stronger than it had been before the first siege. These efforts were not wasted—for an even greater test was coming.

In 1520, Suleiman "The Magnificent" ascended to the throne of the Ottoman Empire. Like Mehmet, he was a man of culture and learning, as well as a brilliant general. Under his leadership, the Ottoman Empire ascended to its greatest heights. One year later, Phillippe Villiers de L'Isle Adam became the Grand Master of the Order of St. John. L'Isle Adam was an educated aristocrat, as well as an experienced seaman and devout Christian. He, too, proved to be a great military leader. The main players were now in place for another one of history's most strategic conflicts.

THE SECOND BATTLE OF RHODES

In 1521, the Sultan sent the newly elected Grand Master a "Letter of Victory" in which he boasted of his recent conquests and asked the Grand Master to "rejoice with me over my triumphs." L'Isle Adam was more direct than diplomatic, and he replied that he understood fully Suleiman's intention to make Rhodes his next conquest. In his next letter, the Sultan curtly demanded that Rhodes be surrendered to him at once.

The Sultan's timing was typically brilliant. Henry VIII of England was in the process of seizing the Order's properties in Britain, while France and Spain were at war, and Italy was impoverished. Once again, the gallant knights could expect no help or reinforcements and only a few hundred of them could be mobilized to take their stand against the most powerful army on earth.

By June of 1522, Suleiman was ready. Historians estimate that he assembled up to 700 ships and 200,000 men for the battle. Even allowing for exaggeration, this was an overwhelming force to come against 500 knights and an estimated 1,500 militiamen. To the world it looked as if the Turks were going sparrow hunting with a cannon. No one expected the knights to last more than a few days against this massive onslaught. On July 28, the Sultan himself landed on Rhodes with a grand salute, and the battle began.

The Turks brought up such a multitude of cannons and mortars that they seemed like a forest. They began a devastating bombardment using siege guns which could hurl cannon balls nine feet in circumference. Throughout the month of August, they poured thousands of these into the city and its fortifications each day. The knights answered with their own artillery, which was much smaller and fewer in number, but quite effective on the relatively unprotected Turks.

By the end of August, a number of breeches began to appear in the fortress walls. A few days later, the first infantry assault began. The knights fought with characteristic resolve, contesting every foot of ground. Even so, the numbers were so overwhelming that the defenders were pushed back until finally the Turks were able to plant their standards on the wall. This had never happened to the knights before, but instead of discouraging them, it gave them even more determination. The knights shocked the Turks with a counterattack, and even the Grand Master entered the fray. After an epic struggle that lasted throughout the day, the Turks began to fall back.

Immediately the Sultan responded by sending a second wave, led by Mustapha Pasha himself, one of the greatest of the Ottoman generals. For two more hours the battle raged on the walls. When the smoke cleared, the knights were still standing, and the Turks were retreating in disarray. The ground was almost completely covered by dead or wounded Turks, but miraculously the knights lost only three men, along with an undetermined number of militiamen.

The Sultan was stunned, disconcerted, and angry. He ordered a continuous bombardment for three straight weeks. On September 24, another great assault was thrown against the crumbling fortress walls. The bastion of Aragon, one of the city's main fortifications, fell to a massive assault by the Janissaries, now fanatically brave after having borne for forty years the humiliation from their previous defeats. It looked as if the end of the knights had finally come. Suleiman had a conqueror's throne set on a raised platform so that he could witness his day of triumph. The battle roared all along the walls of the city as wave after wave of Turks poured out of their trenches in what appeared to be an irresistible tide of death.

However, the end did not come as quickly as expected. All day long, the battle continued to rage. The knights, gleaming in their armor, always seemed to appear wherever the fighting was the thickest. L'Isle Adam could usually be found with his standard-bearer behind him at the most desperate points of conflict. He was the man whom the Turks most wanted to kill, and his standard-bearer helped to mark him as a special target. Yet, those who witnessed this great battle said there was special protection around him that the Turks simply could not penetrate. After one of the bloodiest days that the great Turkish army had ever experienced, the seemingly invincible attack began to waver. Then it crumbled into a wholesale retreat.

DEFEAT WITH HONOR

The astonished Suleiman came down from his elevated throne humiliated and outraged. He immediately condemned to death his two most able generals, but later recanted after being persuaded that it would only serve the side of the Christians. The losses for the knights were great, with 200 killed and an equal number wounded. The losses for the Turks were staggering. Their bodies lay in heaps all around the city. Again, the great siege guns were brought up, and the Sultan poured deadly fire into the walls and streets of the city for two solid months.

The knights were now few in number and weary beyond what they thought their human bodies could endure. Even so, they stayed at their positions, each day looking for the assault that would probably end it all. They knew that the Turkish army was so huge it would eventually prevail. The gallant knights had withstood the most powerful and determined army on earth for nearly five months without receiving reinforcements or provisions. Even though they knew that they would be overwhelmed, they determined to die rather than surrender.

As the siege wore on, the Sultan's disposition toward the knights began to change. He respected courage, and he had never witnessed the kind of valor that the knights had displayed. On Christmas Eve, Suleiman's rising respect for the Order moved him to make an extraordinary offer of peace with honor to the remaining knights. After paying tribute to their courage and endurance, he gave them food and provided his own ships to carry them to the destination of their choice. The knights knew that they were too weak to withstand another assault, and this would at least enable them to fight another day. They accepted.

After meeting with L'Isle Adam, Suleiman reportedly said to his Grand Vizier, "It saddens me to be compelled to force this brave old man to leave his home." The knights received the Sultan's hospitality and sailed away.

Two thousand men had taken their stand against as many as 200,000. The world again marveled as they held their ground for more than six months. The knights endured the greatest bombardment and infantry assaults the world had ever seen. When hearing news of the final fall of Rhodes, Charles V of France stated, "Nothing in the world was ever so well lost as Rhodes."

The knights, who had already gained the respect of the world, were now admired even more. For a time, every nation on earth would salute the standard of the Order of St. John, becoming the only standard in history to gain such universal respect. Even so, their exploits were not over.

Part 2
Prevail or Perish

A New Home, A New Battle

For more than 200 years, the knights had lived on Rhodes, and now they had no home. They were offered a small, relatively inhospitable island in the middle of the Mediterranean, named Malta. They accepted it, and immediately started turning the sleepy little sheep fields into a fortress upon which the future of Europe would soon depend.

Years before, while harbored from a storm on a ship at Malta, lightning struck the sword of L'Isle Adam, reducing it to ashes. This was now considered a providential sign. It was also remembered that the great apostle Paul had once been shipwrecked on this little island, which he also turned into a great victory for the faith. They could not have known that for centuries to come, because of their valor, the very name "Malta" would become a synonym for courage and the Order of St. John would become known as the "Knights of Malta."

With Rhodes in his possession, the Sultan now seemed free to sweep across Europe with little opposition. It must have seemed most improbable to anyone that the battered knights would again bar his path. However, the little Order of St. John would not only rise to challenge them, but would strike the blow that would actually begin the unraveling of the entire Ottoman Empire. Although the Order was severely reduced in both numbers and wealth after their departure from Rhodes, their greatest possessions—determination and courage—were still intact.

The "victory" at Rhodes had been very costly to the Ottomans. Thousands of their finest troops had been killed or badly wounded, but even more importantly for an army, their confidence was badly shaken by the way so few withstood so many for so long. Still, Christian Europe seemed to be an easy prey for the Sultan. The Reformation had broken the Roman Church's domination over Europe and internal struggles were rising everywhere. Centuries of resentment toward Rome, and competition between Protestant movements boiled over into a host of conflicts. Christians were taking up arms against one another and a house so divided could be easily conquered.

Though almost every nation in Europe was at war to some degree with at least one neighbor, and the Order of St. John itself was composed of noblemen from these many different nations, they were able to maintain a remarkable unity in their own ranks. They remained focused on what they considered to be the real enemy and the greatest threat to their faith—Islam.

As soon as the knights arrived on Malta, they began building fortifications and ships from which they could again raid Muslim shipping. It was at this time that the famous Muslim pirate, Barbarossa, was appointed High Admiral of the Turkish fleet. He built the Ottoman navy into a force, and great sea battles began to rage from one end of the Mediterranean to the other. Most of these battles were indecisive, but they kept the world on the edge of its seat. A significant Ottoman naval victory would almost certainly be the beginning of the end for Christian Europe. Again it was the tenacious seafaring Knights of St. John who would stand in the path of such a Turkish victory. Again, the knights were making themselves odious to the Turkish high command.

CHANGING OF THE GUARD

In 1546, Barbarossa died and Dragut assumed command of the increasingly powerful Turkish navy. In 1550, the knights defeated his fleet at Mahdia. For revenge, Dragut attacked Malta. The island was still relatively unfortified, but the few defenders put up such stiff resistance that Dragut had to abandon the attack. Both sides knew that the Turks would come back to Malta.

In 1557, L'Isle Adam died and Jean Parisot de laValette became Grand Master of the Order of St. John. Educated and aristocratic, laValette had once been captured by the Turks and made a galley slave for four years. He was sixty-three years old when he became Grand Master, and he would prove to be a great leader like both L'Isle Adam and d'Abusson before him.

Although Dragut's first raid on Malta was beaten back, it was a sure sign that the knights had again made themselves abhorrent to the Sultan. Suleiman had stretched his empire to its greatest limits, and was preparing for what appeared to be a final assault on Europe. He was not happy about having to deal with the knights again, but they were creating such havoc with his lines of supply that they could not be ignored. Even though they were fewer in number and farther away, they were becoming an increasing threat to his plans. Even though Dragut's raid failed, his reconnaissance of the tiny island's defenses would be valuable for the invasion.

The Sultan was also pressured by the fact that the whole Muslim world was now demanding the destruction of the Order of St. John. At times Suleiman had been enraged by the knights, and at other times he feared them, knowing they could not be defeated without great cost. Finally public opinion forced his hand, and on May 18, 1565, the Turkish fleet was sighted by the watchman in Fort St. Elmo on the edge of Malta.

THE BATTLE FOR MALTA

The Ottoman fleet approaching Malta was a mighty one indeed. It appeared as if an entire forest of spars was moving across the sea. Not until the great Spanish Armada sailed against England would the world see a more powerful fleet assembled. With them came seemingly endless multitudes of the Sultan's finest Janissaries, regulars, and more than 4,000 Iayalars—religious fanatics who sought death over life. This Turkish force came to attack 540 knights, 1,000 foot soldiers, and a little more than 3,000 Maltese militiamen.

The knights again faced what appeared to be impossible odds and their enemy was more determined than ever to win. This time the knights did not even have enough men to try and hold the invaders at the beachhead. Unlike Rhodes, where there was only one fortified city, on Malta the knights were spread out over several forts and cities. Military strategists considered this a serious disadvantage, but it also required the Turks to spread out their forces. Just as those before him had excelled, the new Grand Master was brilliant at maximizing the advantage of every favorable condition, as well as creating the best possible strategies from unfavorable situations.

Almost immediately, the Order's cavalry began attacking and harassing the Turkish foraging parties. This became a major distraction for the Turks, whose previous experiences with the knights were now causing them to overreact in almost every situation. Then the high command, again led by the brilliant Mustapha Pasha, made the strategic mistake of concentrating its main attack on the Post of Castile, possibly the strongest point of the knights' defenses.

This Turkish blunder was the result of the bravery of a single knight, a Frenchman named Adrien de laRiviere, who was captured early in the assault. Under torture, de laRiviere asserted that the Post of Castile was lightly fortified with a small garrison of men, and could be easily taken. After a number of assaults were mauled by the Post of Castile's defenders, Pasha realized that de laRiviere had lied to him. He had the Frenchman beaten to death, but the deception had already cost him hundreds of his fighters. Even more importantly, the confidence of his troops was severely shaken.

ST. ELMO'S FIRE

Pasha then redirected the main part of his force toward capturing St. Elmo, the small fort which overlooked the Grand Harbor. This also played into the hands of the knights as it gave laValette time to make improvements in his other fortifications. Even so, it was apparent that St. Elmo could not hold out for long. The indiscriminate gunfire of the Turks' earlier sieges at Rhodes had now been replaced by mathematical precision and accuracy. Pasha turned his main artillery on the fort with unrelenting fire both day and night. Soon little St. Elmo was crumbling.

One night while in his council chamber in Fort St. Angelo, laValette was disturbed by an unwelcome delegation. A few knights had slipped out of St. Elmo and made their way to laValette to tell him that St. Elmo could no longer hold out. LaValette, a hero at Rhodes, derided the younger knights as unworthy of their fathers. He told the delegation that they need not go back to St. Elmo, but that he would handpick a delegation to relieve them.

Under his scorn, the little troop from St. Elmo begged that they be allowed to return to their post, which laValette finally permitted. As soon as they departed, the Grand Master told the council that he knew the little fort was doomed, but they had to buy more time if the rest were to have a chance.

By now so much smoke and fire was rising from St. Elmo that it looked like a volcano spewing out of the rock. It seemed impossible that anyone in it could still be alive, but the young knights in the little fort were holding their ground, repulsing every attack to the astonishment of both sides, and the outright dismay of the Turks.

Then the famed Dragut arrived with a fresh squadron of ships and even more reinforcements, many of them handpicked fighting men. If Pasha was courageous and brilliant, Dragut was even more so. His presence raised the morale of the entire Turkish force at a time when it was badly needed. Dragut assumed personal command of the forces. He directed more batteries to pour their deadly fire into St. Elmo, which the tiny fort was now receiving from three sides. He relentlessly continued this barrage for three entire weeks. At the end, neither side believed that anyone could have survived in the little fort that was now just a heap of rubble.

When the guns ceased firing, the Janissaries began their assault, confident of a very quick victory, even if they were met with any resistance. To the amazement of both sides, the attack was repulsed, and the Janissaries suffered heavy casualties. Enraged, Dragut brought up almost every battery they had, and began a bombardment so heavy that the entire island shook as if by an earthquake.

The next day, Dragut sent a second massive assault against the little fort with the Iayalars preceding the Janissaries. St. Elmo actually disappeared under the cloud of dust, smoke, and fire. Hours later when the smoke finally cleared, the knights on St. Angelo and St. Michaels, as well as the Turks, marveled as they saw the Cross of St. John still flying above the crumbled ruins. LaValette was so moved, he dispatched a relief force of some of his best fighters to the little fort, but the Muslim forces encircling it were too strong and they had to turn back. The brave little garrison at St. Elmo was now abandoned to its own fate.

The following day, Dragut continued to intensify the bombardment of St. Elmo. There were now fewer than 100 knights left in the fort and nearly all of them were wounded. When the bombardment stopped, the Muslim Imams were heard calling the faithful to either conquer or die for Islam. Wave after wave of the best fighters in the Sultan's army threw themselves at the tiny fort that was now little more than a great pile of rubble. The remaining knights moved into the breach. Those who were too weak to stand asked to be carried into the fray so that they could confront the "infidels" one last time. They fought well and stood their ground until the last knight fell.

St. Elmo's Victory

The little fortress that no one believed could hold out for more than a day or two, withstood for more than a month. This bought the rest of the Order precious time. Little St. Elmo had also deprived the Sultan of thousands of his best fighting men, including many of his leaders. Among the fallen was the master gunner, the Aga of the Janissaries, and most importantly of all, Dragut himself was felled by a cannon shot.

As the Muslim standard was finally raised over the ruins of St. Elmo, Pasha realized that his whole strategy had been wrong. The price paid for St. Elmo had been too great. As he looked up at the larger St. Angelo, whose guns were already pouring a deadly fire into his advancing troops, he cried out, "Allah! If so small a son has cost so dear, what price shall we have to pay for so large a father?"

Pasha then had the bodies of the knights who had died so bravely at St. Elmo decapitated, bound to crosses, and floated out into the harbor in front of St. Angelo. This was a brazen insult to the religion of the defenders. LaValette also understood this meant that there would be no quarter given—this was a fight to the death. In retaliation, laValette had a number of the Turkish prisoners executed and their bodies hung on the walls. Both sides had declared that there would be no terms of peace such as had been given at Rhodes. The knights would prevail on Malta or they would perish.

The remaining fortresses of the knights were now caught in a deadly crossfire from the horrendous artillery bombardments. Pasha intermittently released ground assaults at different points of the defenses, seeking to achieve a single breach. Each attack turned into a massacre for his troops. Pasha finally maneuvered his forces until they encircled laValette's headquarters. He then released such a bombardment upon it that the inhabitants of the islands of Syracuse and Catania, seventy and one hundred miles away, heard the roar of the guns.

When the barrage finally stopped, Pasha sent a massive assault swarming over the walls. A breach was finally made and the Turkish general poured his troops into it. A mighty struggle raged for more than six hours, but the knights somehow closed the gap and retook the walls. Mortified, Pasha tore his beard and called off the assault. Again, the endurance and tenacity of the Order had been seriously underestimated.

A SURPRISING RETREAT

Pasha then escalated his bombardment to the point where it seemed the barrels of his cannon would melt, and he kept it up for seven more days. Then he released another assault, sending thousands upon thousands into the fray. The Order was so reduced in number that the breach was made quickly. The knights fought bravely, but they were simply far too outnumbered to stand against so great a tide of raging humanity. Just when the citadel itself was within reach of the Turks and it appeared that the end of the knights had finally arrived, the Ottoman trumpets rang out a call for a full-scale retreat!

The defenders could only believe that the continent had finally sent them relief, but this was not the case. What had actually happened was that a small force of the

Order's cavalry had attacked the Ottoman base camp at Marsa. The little detachment had struck with such fierce determination and raised so much havoc that they were mistaken for a much larger force. Fearing an attack from the rear, Pasha had been forced to call a retreat of his assault troops.

When he learned he had been deceived at the very moment when victory was within his grasp, his rage knew no bounds. He redoubled the artillery, releasing continuous bombardment day and night that wore on until it seemed improbable for any living thing to survive inside the fortress walls.

A council of knights recommended a withdrawal be made from all of the outposts into the single fortress of St. Angelo. However, Grand Master laValette adamantly refused, vowing again that he would not surrender an acre to the infidels. Military historians later agreed that his tenacity in holding every fortified point probably saved the knights, because it kept the Turks from massing at any one location.

LaValette received a dispatch from Don Garcia of Sicily, promising to send a relief force of 16,000 men. LaValette was unimpressed. Having received many such promises before, he did not put his trust in princes. He simply vowed again to fight until victory or death came.

FIRE FROM BELOW

The Turks had not only been pouring their deadly fire into the city over its walls, but they had also spent weeks tunneling under them. On August 18, a mine exploded under the Post of Castile and a great breach was made. The Grand Master himself, now seventy years old, grabbed a helmet and sword and rushed out to meet the assault. The knights and townspeople, encouraged by his example, picked up any weapon they could find and flung themselves into the breach with him. LaValette was wounded but refused to retreat. He pointed his sword at the Turkish banners and declared, "Never will I withdraw as long as those banners wave in the wind." Somehow the knights again prevailed, and the Turks once again bitterly retreated.

Dissensions now began to arise within the ranks of the Turkish High Command. The battle they had projected would take only a few days had now lasted months, and there was still no end in sight. Pasha began to calculate how he could get enough supplies from Tripoli, Greece, or Constantinople to keep up the siege through the winter. He seemed to know that if they did not prevail here it would be the "high water mark" of the great Ottoman Empire. He was right.

On September 6, Don Garcia's fleet arrived with 8,000 reinforcements. Even though 8,000 was not a significant number compared to the still huge army of the Turks, their impact on the morale of both sides was much greater than the strength of their numbers. If a few hundred knights had cost them so dearly, and they had only captured the little fort of St. Elmo, how could they possibly prevail against so many more? The great army of the mighty Ottoman Empire struck camp and sailed away. This was to be their high water mark, and the tide of this great empire would now begin to recede like every empire before it. The little Order of St. John stood against the seemingly innumerable hordes of Islam and turned them back.

The Sultan's army returned to the Golden Horn with fewer than a third of his troops.

Suleiman was disbelieving. He insisted that his fleet come into the harbor under the cover of darkness so the people would not see its terrible state. He then remarked, "I now see that it is only in my own hand that my sword is invincible." He immediately planned to lead another expedition to Malta the following year, but like Mehmet before him, Suleiman did not live to fulfill this vow.

EUROPE CELEBRATES

For a second time, the great general Pasha, head of the most powerful army in the world, was defeated by a few hundred "warrior monks." The world again marveled at those "archaic relics from the past," who stood almost entirely alone against the greatest military threat to ever arise against Europe. In one of the greatest examples of courage and endurance the world has ever witnessed, the Knights of St. John prevailed. Only 250 knights survived at Malta and almost every one of them was wounded, maimed, or crippled for life. Europe, however, was now free of the Muslim threat that had appeared so invincible.

In England, where Henry VIII had confiscated the Order's property, Queen

Elizabeth acknowledged that if Malta had fallen to the Turks, England itself would probably have fallen to the Muslims. She ordered the Archbishop of Canterbury to appoint a special form of thanksgiving to be read in every church in the land each day for three weeks. The rest of Europe also celebrated, paying their respects and acknowledging their debt to the Order that had long before been written off as having no real value.

While the Christian nations of Europe had turned their armies against each other, the Knights of St. John never lost sight of who their real enemy was. Even though the Order was composed of noble sons from the Christian nations that were fighting each other, they never allowed doctrinal or political divisions to enter their own ranks. Because of their unity, focused vision, and determination never to retreat before the enemies of the cross, they changed forever what had appeared to be the inevitable course of history. Due to their extraordinary exploits, the standard of the Knights of St. John, now called "the Maltese Cross," were for a time saluted by every nation in the world.

Part 3
Last Day Knights

THE CONTINUING HISTORY OF THE SOVEREIGN ORDER OF ST. JOHN OF JERUSALEM, RHODES, AND MALTA

After the Battle of Malta, the Order was held in high esteem among Christian nations of Europe. However, as Islam ceased to be a threat to Europe, the valiant deeds of the Order were soon forgotten. Some European rulers even considered the knights to be a danger to their sovereignty, and sought to weaken the Order by confiscating their property. The Order also went through some periods of its own debauchery. Yet each time this occurred, a new leader arose, brought repentance, and restored the vision of living by the highest standards of chivalry, honor, and Christian virtues. Even so, the tests that came from the nations they fought so hard to protect would prove to be just as great as those that came from Islam. Staying true to their vow not to take up arms against other Christians, the Order began to weaken and shrink, but somehow they always found a way to survive.

Because the Order was composed mostly of noblemen it became a special target of the French Revolution, which was fueled mostly by the determination of its leaders to destroy the French nobility. During this time, the Order's most valuable properties were confiscated. In 1798, Napoleon Bonaparte landed on Malta on his way to Egypt with a massive invading force. After offering token resistance, the Order elected to leave their beloved Malta rather than break their vow not to take up arms against the forces of another Christian nation. Napoleon left Malta after a few days, carrying aboard his flagship priceless treasures which were seized from the Order. This ship was eventually sunk by British forces in Egyptian waters with the treasure still on board.

The Order was devastated by the loss of Malta, and it began to fracture as many of the knights felt that the apparently anti-Christian Napoleon should have been resisted with the same zeal with which they had resisted Islam. The French Revolution was also ruthlessly anti-Christian, and some even considered Napoleon to be the anti-christ. The remaining knights drifted through Europe, seeking a new home and a new vision. They found both in Russia.

A treaty was signed between the Order and Russian Emperor Paul I. The Czar was recognized as the Protector of the Order. Eventually, he was elected Grand Master, and the Order's insignia was officially added to the Imperial Coat-of-Arms. The statutes of the Order were then reconstructed to meet the requirements of the times, allowing those who were worthy from other denominational backgrounds to be invested as knights. This was done so that Russian noblemen, who were generally of the Russian Orthodox tradition, could be included. At the same time, hereditary knighthood was conferred upon the sons of noblemen.

Pope Pius VI sent a letter to the Czar expressing his appreciation that the Czar had become the Sovereign Protector of the Order, apparently also giving his approval for the inclusion of those from other Christian denominations. Historians have interpreted this as the Pope's acknowledgment of the legitimacy of the Order's new ecumenical direction. In 1879, an exclusively Roman Catholic Order was commissioned by Pope Leo XIII, and then claimed to be the only legitimate Order of St. John. Of course this was disputed by the ecumenical Order, which still included many Roman Catholics.

A number of the hereditary knights came to the new world and in 1908 founded an American Grand Priory which received Legal Charter in 1911. A Grand Priory of Canada was also established in the ecumenical and nonpolitical tradition. Today the Grand Priory of Canada operates under a charter granted by the Government of Canada as "The Sovereign Order of St. John, of Jerusalem, Rhodes, and Malta." The Sovereign Order is now recognized as the world's oldest, continuing Order of Chivalry and its headquarters have been reestablished in Malta.

COURAGEOUS KNIGHTS IN THE LAST-DAY CHURCH

With little fanfare, knights of the Order are still active and doing exploits in defense of the Christian faith, preserving truth and honor, and continuing their devotion to serving "our lords, the poor and the sick."

Each Knight of Malta dedicates himself to Christian service and humility. He wears the eightpointed cross of Malta and receives the title of "Chevalier" upon being accepted as a knight. The motto of the Order is: "AS WE ARE UNITED IN CHRIST, WE ARE UNITED WITH ONE ANOTHER."

Applicants for knighthood must be practicing and exemplary Christians, active in their church, and doing charitable works in their community. They must be ready to help those in need, such as the sick, the orphans, and the aged. They must be men of honor, who stand for truth without compromise.

Like the nation of Israel, the Order of St. John the Baptist seems to have been uniquely preserved to play a part in the final battle between light and darkness. The church, and even Western civilization, are no less in jeopardy today than they were during the time of Suleiman. Conflicts within the church have weakened her to the point where she is more vulnerable than ever to the enemy. Even so, the Lord is not constrained to deliver by many or by few. He still has those who are true noblemen, establishing noble families throughout the earth. They are bound together by a common faith that transcends denominational differences. They, too, have vowed never to retreat before the enemies of the cross, nor to yield a single acre of ground to the enemy of their faith.

The Lord again is calling together true knights of the Spirit who will stand unified in spite of all the petty divisions and spiritual wars that surround them. Aware of the real enemy, they too, will stand without wavering against the greatest darkness of their times and will push the darkness back. Some are in the modern Order of St. John. Some may be in your church. One of them may even be you.

THE PRESENT ORDER OF ST. JOHN

In the Yearbook of Italian Nobility (1883), it is recorded that the family Cumbo is of Spanish origin, having emigrated to Sicily, Reggio Calabria (Italy) and Malta in about 1300. In the Book of Sicilian Nobility (1912), it is recorded that the name Cumbo belongs to an ancient and noble Italian family which possessed baronial lands in Bonalbergo and enjoyed the rank of nobility. The arrival of the Cumbo family in Malta (around 1600) is attributed to three brothers, Enrico, Ruggiero, and Andrea. In 1698 the family added the name Frendo, becoming known as Frendo Cumbo. The Grand Master's ancestors held high offices as Barons in the King's Court.

H.E. Count Joseph Frendo Cumbo is retired from both the British and Canadian military, having served in Malta, the Middle East, Italy, Sudan, Palestine, East Africa, and North Africa. He served in the British Army as a career soldier from 1939 to 1956, with duties such as infantryman, air-dispatcher, and paratrooper.

After emigrating to Canada, he served in the Ontario Regiment (Tanks) for several years as a Squadron Sergeant Major, earned the Canadian Forces Decoration & Clasp, and served as the Guard Sergeant Major at Ottawa in 1967 during the Queen's visit for the celebrations of the Centennial year. Later he became a commissioned officer and served in the Canadian Navy Reserve as the Commanding Officer of the Sea Cadets, retiring with the rank of Captain (SEA). Military Decorations; 193945 Star, Africa Star, Italy Star, Defense Medal, Victory Medal, Palestine (GSM) 194548, Canadian Forces Decoration & Clasp, the Polonia Restituta and the Polish Gold Cross of Merit.

He is the holder of various decorations and knighthoods, including the Order of Military of St. Agatha de Paterno, the Royal Balearic Crown, Holy Sepulchre, and others. In the Sovereign Order of St. John of Jerusalem, Knights of Malta, he has been the Prior of Canada and since 1974, the Grand Prior.

H.E. The Grand Master of the Sovereign Order of St. John

Deputy for the Commonwealth

Capt. J. Frendo Cumbo, C.D. (RTD)

Marquis & Count De Torre Sarroca

GCSJ, MOC, ORCB, KHS; (h.c.) PH.D, D.HUM, D.Re, CSM

Bailiff Grand Cross of Justice

Hereditary Knight, OSJ

Member of the Supreme Council

Ambassador Royal House of Aragon, N. America

BIBLIOGRAPHY

Achievement of the Knights of Malta,
by Alexander Sutherland, Published 1846,
2 Volumes.

*History of Malta During the Period of the
French and English Occupation,*
by William Hardman, London 1909

History of the Knights of Malta,
by Major Whitworth Porter, 2 Volumes,
London, 1858.

The House of the Temple,
by Frederick Ryan, London, 1930.

The Knights of the Order,
by Ernie Bradford, (Dorset Press).

Malta of the Knights,
by E.W. Schermerhorn, England, 1929.

The Order of St. John,
by Count Joseph Frendo Cumbo.

Ordre Souverain de St. Jean de Jerusalem,
Imprimerie Imperial, Saint Petersburg,
Russia, 1800.